Animal Classifications

Reptiles

Angela Royston

Raintree is an imprint of Capstone Global Library Limited, a company incorporated in England and Wales having its registered office at 7 Pilgrim Street, London, EC4V 6LB – Registered company number: 6695582

www.raintree.co.uk
myorders@raintree.co.uk

Edited by Helen Cox Cannons, Clare Lewis and
        Abby Colich
Designed by Steve Mead
Picture research by Tracy Cummins
Production by Victoria Fitzgerald
Originated by Capstone Global Library Ltd
Printed and bound in China

ISBN 978 1 406 28741 7 (hardback)
18 17 16 15 14
10 9 8 7 6 5 4 3 2 1

ISBN 978 1 406 28748 6 (paperback)
19 18 17
10 9 8 7 6 5 4 3 2

British Library Cataloguing in Publication Data
A full catalogue record for this book is available from the British Library.

Acknowledgements
We would like to thank the following for permission to reproduce photographs: Getty Images: Mint Images, 26; iStockphotos: © GJohnson2, 22; Photoshot: Jeff Simon, 18; Shutterstock: ANDRZEJ GRZEGORCZYK, 16, Audrey Snider-Bell, 25, Cathy Keifer, 12, CreativeNature.nl, 27, David Evison, 20, 28, Delmas Lehman, 11, Heiko Kiera, 19, holbox, 10, Jonald Morales, 15, Kjeld Friis, 7, Kjersti Joergensen, 21, Leena Robinson, 13, 29 Bottom, leungchopan, Cover, Linda Bucklin, 24, Matt Jeppson, 6, Maxim Petrichuk, 4, Melinda Fawver, 17, Morris Mann, 8, PhotoSky, Design Element, Raffaella Calzoni, 5, worldswildlifewonders, 14; SuperStock: Animals Animals, 23, 29 Middle, Tier und Naturfotografie, 9, 29 Top.
We would like to thank Michael Bright for his invaluable help in the preparation of this book.

Every effort has been made to contact copyright holders of material reproduced in this book. Any omissions will be rectified in subsequent printings if notice is given to the publisher.

All the Internet addresses (URLs) given in this book were valid at the time of going to press. However, due to the dynamic nature of the Internet, some addresses may have changed, or sites may have changed or ceased to exist since publication. While the author and publisher regret any inconvenience this may cause readers, no responsibility for any such changes can be accepted by either the author or the publisher.

Contents

Meet the reptiles...4

Body shape 6

Long, bendy snakes 8

Warming up.. 10

Lizards.. 12

Scaly skin.. 14

Turtles and tortoises...................................... 16

Laying eggs 18

Baby turtles.. 20

Young reptiles.. 22

Great survivors... 24

One amazing reptile!..................................... 26

Quiz... 28

Glossary 30

Find out more.. 31

Index.. 32

Some words are shown in bold, **like this.** You can find out what they mean by looking in the glossary.

Meet the reptiles

Reptiles are a large group of animals, which include lizards, snakes, turtles, alligators and crocodiles. Scientists divide living things into groups. This is called **classification**.

Many lizards live in hot places. They even live in deserts.

Alligators live in rivers and swamps. Watch out for their sharp teeth!

Each group is different from other groups in particular ways. All reptiles have dry skin, which is covered in **scales**, and they keep warm by taking in heat from their surroundings.

Body shape

Reptiles belong to a larger group of animals called **vertebrates**. Like humans and other **mammals**, they have a **skeleton** made of bones. Their backbone is made of many smaller, knobbly bones.

A snake has a very long backbone!

A turtle swims by using its legs as paddles or flippers to pull it through the water.

Most reptiles have four legs, which they use to move on land and in water. Snakes have no legs. They move by bending their bodies into an "S" shape and pushing back against the ground.

Long, bendy snakes

Snakes use their long, bendy bodies in many ways. They **coil** up their bodies to rest and to sleep. Tree snakes wind and slither through the branches of trees.

A tree snake coils its body over a branch.

Anacondas can grow to great lengths.

Snakes such as pythons and anacondas wrap their bodies around **prey** and then squeeze them to death. Other snakes kill their prey with **venom,** which they inject through their **fangs.**

Warming up

Most reptiles are **cold blooded**. This means that they cannot make their own heat, as birds and **mammals** do. Instead, they take in heat from their surroundings.

A lizard warms up quickly by basking in the sunshine.

An alligator may slide into the river to cool down on a hot day.

When reptiles are cold, they move very slowly. As they warm up, they move around much faster. In parts of the world with cold winters, many reptiles make a **burrow** and **hibernate**.

Lizards

Lizards like hot places and many live in deserts. Once they have warmed up they move fast, catching insects to eat. If they get too hot, they move into the shade or under a rock to cool down.

This chameleon has an extremely long tongue for catching insects.

tongue

This green anole is a lizard. It can change the colour of its skin to match its surroundings.

Many lizards are brightly coloured. Some lizards blend in with their surroundings. This is called **camouflage**. They may also change colour when they are angry!

Scaly skins

A reptile's skin is covered with hard **scales**. The scales are waterproof and stop the reptile's body from drying out. Crocodiles have large, heavy scales, but lizards and snakes have much smaller ones.

A crocodile has a tough, thick skin. Its back is protected by hard plates, like armour.

A snake's skin can have different colours and patterns.

The scales on a snake's skin do not grow as the snake grows. When the skin gets too small, the snake wriggles out of it, revealing a new skin underneath.

Turtles and tortoises

Turtles and tortoises are even better protected than crocodiles. The skin is covered with thick **scales,** which join together to make the shell that you see.

A giant tortoise measures up to 1.3 metres (4 feet) long.

A tortoise's shell is smooth and shiny.

Tortoises and some turtles can pull their legs and head into the shell. Then their whole body is protected.

Laying eggs

A reptile begins life inside an egg. Some reptiles make a hole in the ground, like a nest, and lay their eggs in it. Most reptiles' eggs have a bendy, leathery shell, but crocodiles, tortoises and some geckoes lay eggs with hard shells.

American alligators lay their eggs in a mound of rotting plants.

This young python is beginning to hatch.

A baby reptile has a special egg tooth.
When it is ready to **hatch**, the baby uses its
egg tooth to cut its way out of the shell.

Baby turtles

Although turtles live in the ocean, they lay their eggs on land. The mother turtle lays her eggs on a beach, out of reach of the sea. She covers them with sand before she returns to the sea.

A female turtle digs a hole in the sand for her eggs.

Lots of baby turtles hatch at the same time. They run across the sand to reach the sea.

When the eggs **hatch,** the tiny turtles rush down the beach to the sea. Many are snapped up by hungry birds before they reach the water.

Young reptiles

Most young reptiles have to look after themselves from the moment they **hatch**. Only a few survive to become adults. The rest are caught by **predators,** such as birds and other reptiles.

Young baby snakes have to find their own food and try to avoid being eaten.

These baby alligators ride safely through the water on their mother's head!

Crocodiles and alligators look after their young. When young Nile crocodiles hatch, their mother carries them in her mouth to the water.

Great survivors

Reptiles have survived on Earth for a very long time. Dinosaurs were reptiles and were the most powerful animals on Earth for millions of years.

Stegosaurus lived about 150 million years ago. It ate plants and had two rows of bony plates on its back.

Crocodiles first appeared on Earth about 250 million years ago.

Many reptiles that lived at the same time as the dinosaurs died out about 64 million years ago. Crocodiles did not die out and have changed very little.

One amazing reptile!

Tuataras live in the wild on islands off the coast of New Zealand. They have lived on Earth for about 200 million years, almost as long as crocodiles. Tuataras look like lizards, but they are **classified** in a group of their own.

A tuatara is the only living member of its group.

A tuatara has a row of spines along its back.

Tuataras grow very slowly. Young tuataras have a mysterious third eye on top of their heads. It becomes covered by **scales** as they grow into adults.

Quiz

Look at the pictures below and read the clues. Can you remember the names of these reptiles? Look back in the book if you need help.

1. I live in the ocean but lay my eggs on a sandy beach. What am I?

2. I squeeze my **prey** to death. I can grow very long. What am I?

3. I am a baby and my mother takes care of me. What am I?

4. The colour of my skin changes to match my surroundings. What am I?

Glossary

burrow animal's underground home

camouflage when the colour or shape of an animal causes it to blend in with its surroundings

classification system that scientists use to divide living things into separate groups

classified put into a group according to special things shared by that group

coil wind round and round in a circle

cold blooded when an animal is unable to make its own heat and has to take heat from its surroundings

fang long, hollow tooth

hatch break out of an egg

hibernate go into a very deep sleep to survive very cold or very dry weather

mammal animal that has hair and feeds its young with milk from the mother

predator animal that kills other animals for food

prey animal that is hunted by another animal for food

scales small, hard plates that cover an animal's skin

skeleton hard frame that gives vertebrate animals their shape.

venom poison that is injected by a sting or bite

vertebrate animal that has a backbone and skeleton inside its body

Find out more

Books

Remarkable Reptiles (Extreme Animals), Isabel Thomas (Raintree, 2013)

Reptiles, Catriona Clarke (Usborne, 2009)

Reptiles and Amphibians (Deadly Factbook), Steve Backshall (Orion Books, 2013)

Websites

kcc.org.nz/tuatara
This website includes lots of information, fun facts and games about tuataras and other New Zealand wildlife.

kids.nationalgeographic.com/kids/animals/creaturefeature
Learn about lots of different reptiles on this website.

kids.sandiegozoo.org/animals/reptiles
The kids' section of the San Diego Zoo website includes photos and information about reptiles. Click the small photos to find out about particular animals. Don't miss the games, videos and animal cams at the top.

Index

alligators 4, 5, 11, 18, 23
anacondas 9

baby reptiles 19, 20–23, 27
backbones 6
birds 10, 21, 22
body shape 6–7
burrows 11

camouflage 13
chameleons 12
classification 4, 26
cold blooded 10
colours 13, 15
crocodiles 4, 14, 18, 23, 25

dinosaurs 24, 25

egg tooth 19
eggs 18–19, 20–21

fangs 9

geckoes 18
green anoles 13
hatch 19, 21, 22
hibernation 11

lizards 4, 10, 12–13, 14

mammals 6, 10

predators 21, 22
prey 9, 12
pythons 9, 19

scales 5, 14–15, 16, 27
shells 16–17
skeletons 6
snakes 4, 6, 7, 8–9, 14, 15, 19, 22
Stegosaurus 24

tortoises 16–17, 18
tree snakes 8
tuataras 26–27
turtles 4, 7, 16–17, 20–21

venom 9
vertebrates 6

warming up 5, 10–11, 12